THE ADVENTURES OF TINY THE BEAR

BY POP POP

ILLUSTRATED BY THE DOOHAN SISTERS
COLLEEN: BRIDGETTE: KATIE: KELSEY:

1st Printing
2010

Funtasy Publications
220 Sleepy Creek Rd
Macon GA 31210 USA

funtasypublications.com

goodnews.netministries.org

davidwaltersministry.com

Table Of Contents

Tiny the Bear's First Adventure _____ Page   6

Tiny the Bear Has Another Adventure_____ Page   9

Tiny the Bear Has More Adventures _____ Page 19

Tiny and Stuffy Open a Shop _____ Page 29

Market Day for the Bears _____Page 39

Tiny The Bear Gives Some Wise Advise _____ Page 44

Tiny & Stuffy Have A Special Party_____ Page 56

Epilogue _____Page 68

Wee Willie Wannabe _____Page 71

Introduction

I would like to introduce the readers to 'Tiny the Bear.'
As stories of bears and toy bears are very popular with
children, such as *Teddy Bears, Care Bears, Winnie the
Pooh, Paddington Bear, Rupert Bear and the Berenstain
Bears.* I believe Tiny will find his place amongst these
famous bears.

Tiny is a grizzly bear, but he was born in the fantasy
country of Lilliput where Gulliver was shipwrecked, on
his travels, so he looks very small compared with the
bears of our world.

Even though he is small and quite young , he is a very
wise and clever bear. The unique thing about Tiny is that
he converses with people, usually children, as well as
with other bears and he has a habit of befriended them.
He also shows children how they can succeed
even when circumstances are stacked against them.

Enjoy Tiny's adventures in this illustrated book.

Pop Pop.

Other Books by Pop Pop

The Book Of Funtastic Adventures

The 2nd Book Of Funtastic Adventures

Audio version of
The Book Of Funtastic Adventures

Pop Pop's Grandsons have amazing and hilarious adventures as junior Jedi Knights.

They meet famous cartoon and movie action heroes and also well known book and fairy tale characters.

Available on
amazon.com
goodnews.netministries.com
funtasypublications.com
And in all good bookstores.
Or order direct from
Good News Ministries
220 Sleepy Creek Rd Macon GA 31210
478-757-8071 800-300-0136

Chapter One
Tiny the Bear's First Adventure

Once upon a time there was a grizzly bear called Tiny. No one knows why he was called Tiny, because he was enormous. In fact he was the largest bear in all the Land of Lilliput. It was believed that he got his name from the Land of Giants. It was probably that being a Lilliputian bear the giants saw him and he was tiny in their sight so they called him `Tiny'. Lilliput is where Gulliver traveled to where all the people were only about six inches tall. Also Jedi Zion and Jedi Judah traveled there in Pop Pop's book. *"The Book of Funtastic Adventures."*

One day Tiny went for a tiny walk to have a tiny adventure. He brought a tiny jar of honey with him to have a tiny picnic. He sat down by a tiny tree and while he was enjoying his tiny jar of honey, (Well he wasn't really enjoying the tiny jar, but the tiny honey inside the jar.) there came a tiny shower of rain. He thought, "This tiny shower will make me `Tiny' a tiny bit wet."

Just at that time a boy came up to him and said, `Tiny will you please eat me?'

"You are not a Lilliputian, you are real big and it would take me about two years to eat you up. And I am already full. For my tiny tummy is full of tiny honey. And why do you want me to eat you?"

"Because I'm Flippin Awful."

"I can see that," said Tiny.

"You don't understand," replied the boy. "Flippin is my first name and Awful is my last name, and I really live up to it. Every time I mess up, my Mom says to me Flippin Awful you are flippin awful." When I go to school the teacher says Flippin Awful your grades are Flippin awful. And all the kids flippin laugh at me. In fact they flippin well laugh at me all the time. And it flippin well hurts me, because they are flippin rude.

"What does flippin mean?" asked Tiny.

"It just replaces a bad or cuss word," said Flippin, "English people use it a lot."

"Are you Flippin English then?" asked Tiny. "No! But my mom and dad are," replied Flippin.

"Why is your last name so bad?" asked Tiny. "Because it's awful," replied Flippin.

"What does awful mean then?" asked Tiny who was very clever for a bear.

"Yucky! Disgusting! Stupid! Ugly!"

"If you add just the letter 'E' in the middle of your name it no longer means that. Aweful really means 'full of Awe' and Awe means 'Wonder'. So the real meaning of your last name is, Full of Wonder or Awesome."

"Is that for real?" asked Flippin.

"Absolutely! Remember your name means Flippin Wonderful, so when anyone calls your name or says you are Flippin Aweful take it a complement," advised Tiny. So that little conversation changed the life of Flipping Awful. Don't let other people's opinion or one little letter destroy your dreams. You have the potential to succeed in whatever you want to do.

Chapter Two
Tiny The Bear Has Another Adventure

One sunny morning Tiny the Bear woke up from a long winter sleep. "What a wonderful morning!" Tiny exclaimed as he saw the sun shining and felt a warm breeze blowing. "After I've eaten a tiny jar of tiny honey which I have saved, I will go and have a tiny adventure." So after filling his tiny tummy with some tiny honey off he went looking to see how he could have this tiny adventure.

As Tiny walked along, (well he didn't walk along like people do, for he was a bear so he kind of rumbled along in a tiny manner) he enjoyed seeing all the birds and creatures out and about enjoying themselves. He especially enjoyed seeing the spring flowers, because he knew that the bees would be out soon and that meant he would be able to find plenty of honey to fill up his tiny honey jars.

As Tiny continued his tiny walk in anticipation of a tiny adventure, he was suddenly approached by another bear. This one was quite a bit bigger than Tiny and he looked pretty fierce.
"Hello! My name is Tiny."
Grr! Grr! Growled the other bear.

Tiny meets the Wild Bear who becomes Stuffy

"What's you name? asked Tiny.

"I don't have a name; I'm just a wild bear," he growled back.

"What are you wild about?" asked Tiny politely.

"Because I live in the wild! All bears that live in the wild are wild."

"Why?" asked Tiny.

"I guess we are wild about living in the wild," growled back the wild bear.

"I'm sure it doesn't have to be that way. Just because your parents, grandparents and all your ancestors were wild, doesn't mean you have to be. " replied Tiny.

"So why are you tiny, Tiny? Just because your mom and dad and grandparent were tiny, you don't have to be.' argued the wild bear.

"That's different, I can't do much about my physical size; (anyway I was born in Lilliput and even though I'm Tiny, I'm very fit and strong,) but I can do something about the way I behave. I can change from the inside and I have. And you can do the same," stated Tiny wisely.

"You seem very clever and knowledgeable for a bear." exclaimed the wild bear growling more with curiosity than hostility.

"I guess that's true! I was able to help a big boy who was very depressed about his name. I think I have a large clever brain in my small body, but come to think of it the Lilliputians think I'm enormous," replied Tiny.

"So you think I could become less wild then?"

"Absolutely! Think of the wasted energy you use

up if you're wild all the time," declared Tiny.

"But you have to stay wild to protect yourself from all your enemies that live in the wild," explained the wild bear.

"That's a thought," replied Tiny. "If they all think the same way, then everyone is fighting and killing and eating each other. If they became vegetarians then they wouldn't have to be wild," declared Tiny, feeling very wise and clever for a bear.

"If we all became vegetarians we would fight over the vegetables," explained the wild bear.

"I guess you're right, But we bears mainly eat fish berries and honey and there is plenty to go around, even to share," said Tiny.

"Ok! I will give it a try. Can I join you and share your food?" asked the wild bear.

At this point Tiny became concerned as he wasn't sure if he had or would be able to get enough food for both of them. He thought about telling the wild bear that he didn't want to do that, but then he thought that it could make the wild bear even wilder. Also he was thinking it wouldn't be right to tell this wild bear how to be good, tame and peaceful, without helping him. So he agreed that the wild bear could join him and learn how to become content and peaceful and how to do tiny steps. So off they went together on this tiny adventure, even though Tiny was thinking that perhaps the tiny adventure was now over.

"I'm very hungry and there doesn't seem to be much food around. I hope I don't have to eat you," growled the wild bear to Tiny.

"I'm sure we will find some honey or fish very soon," replied Tiny anxiously. "I also wish that you were not called a wild bear, otherwise you will try to live up to your name. In fact I think it would be wise to rename you and give you a nice name. How about Kind Bear or Stuffed bear." suggested Tiny.

"Why call me Stuffed bear?" Asked the wild bear. "Well, children like stuffed bears!" replied Tiny.

"Why do children like stuffed bears?"

I'm not sure, but I guess that if bears are stuffed then they aren't hungry anymore so they won't eat the children."

"Is that really true?" replied the wild bear.

"I'm not sure, but if we see some children we could asked them," said Tiny thoughtfully.

"Alright! So in the meantime I will be a kind bear and you can call me Stuffy."

So off the two bears went looking for some children to see if they could answer their questions. As far as Tiny was concerned, he felt it was only a tiny question considering that he was on a tiny adventure. He also hoped to see a least one tiny child.

"I'm still very hungry," growled Stuffy "and I don't feel stuffed at all."

"Then we had better find some food soon so you can live up to your new name." said Tiny anxiously.

After a little while, they came across a clearing in the woods. It was beside a small lake and there was lots of green grass and the clearing was surrounded on three

Tiny meets the children

sides by trees. A bunch of children were playing outside some tents. "Maybe we can catch some fish in the lake," growled Stuffy.

"Let me speak to the children first, as you growl too much and you may scare them off," quietly suggested Tiny to Stuffy.

Tiny approached the children and politely asked, "Who are you? "

"Oh My! Oh My! a talking bear. Are you from a circus?" asked one of the children as the others stood there with wide eyes staring at the two bears.

"Well I asked the question first. Who are you?"

"We are children."

"I can see that, but who are you?"

"We are Wigwamers."

"Wigwamers?"

"Yes! Because we are camping in Wigwams and we belong to the Wigwamers' club so we are called Wigwamers," replied all the children together.

"So why do you have your faces painted?" asked Tiny.

"So we can go hunting and go on the warpath," replied one of the little boys.

"What do you hunt?" growled Stuffy.

"Wow! The big one talks as well; in a kind of growley voice," said one of the little girls.

"We hunt deer, rabbits and bears," said an older boy whose face was covered with scary looking war paint.

"So you want to hunt us! We could come and eat you all up right now," growled Stuffy angrily.

The Wigwammers Club

"Oh! We only play. It's make believe. Anyway we wouldn't hunt and eat circus bears," said another little girl.

"But our dads would hunt wild bears!" added a little boy.

"Well it's a good job we are not wild. My name is Tiny and this is my big friend, Stuffy."

"Oh what cute names!" cooed a little girl. "I could take Tiny home as a pet and he could sleep in my bedroom."

"And I could take Stuffy home and he could sleep in my back yard. Then I could take him to school sometimes and scare all the kids with 'show and tell'," said another boy excitedly.

"Thanks all the same, but I don't think that would work," said Tiny.

"I have heard that you children like stuffed bears," growled Stuffy.

"Oh we like all sorts of stuffed animals," said one little girl.

"It must be expensive keeping all your animals stuffed, said Tiny.

"What do you mean?" asked a little boy.

"Once an animal is stuffed, it's not hungry anymore," replied Tiny.

"Especially bears," added Stuffy in his growley voice

"Oh no! Stuffed animals and bears are not real, they are dummies or toy bears and they are stuffed with stuffing. And we like to take them to bed, because they are soft and cuddly.

"What kind of stuffing are they stuffed with?" asked Tiny.

"Just material, like cotton or wool fibers," replied a knowledgeable little girl.

"So now we know why you kids like stuffed bears and other animals," said Tiny.

"I'm hungry do you have any food?" asked Stuffy,

"We can't eat stuffing, but we can eat food; honey preferably," added Tiny.

"Yes! We have a couple of big jars of honey. Would you like some," said all the children together.

"Are you kidding?" replied Stuffy.

"Yes please," said Tiny.

So they all had a picnic together. And I must say that the two bears devoured almost all of the honey in the big jars.

"It was nice meeting you two bears and perhaps you had better leave before the adults return as they don't believe in talking bears and they might want to hunt you," advised one of the bigger children.

So Tiny and Stuffy decided it was time to leave, even though they would have loved to have laid down and taken a nap as they were now very stuffed and sleepy. So off they went at a slower pace, (Stuffy doing tiny steps which was hard for him to do) both looking for a quiet, cozy, safe spot to take their long deserved nap after their tiny adventure.

Chapter Three
Tiny the Bear Has More Adventures.

Tiny and Stuffy had now become good friends, although Tiny wasn't sure if he wanted to take care of Stuffy forever. He didn't want Stuffy to go back and become a wild bear and live in the wild again, but he felt that taking care of Stuffy was becoming too much of a responsibility. Also Stuffy being so much larger than Tiny and having a larger tummy to fill, added to Tiny's problems. Unfortunately, Tiny didn't always have enough food to keep Stuffy happy, so often they both went hungry. The problem was that when Stuffy got really hungry and there wasn't any food available, he became grumpy. In fact Tiny was wondering if he should re-name Stuffy "Grumpy."

"I must think this through and see if I can solve this problem," said Tiny to himself. Being a very clever bear Tiny began to think very hard. In fact he thought so hard that his tiny brain began to give him a tiny headache. "Ooh! All this thinking doesn't come easy," he cried.

During this time Stuffy was taking one of his long naps, so he didn't know what Tiny was trying to sort out.

Suddenly Tiny stood up on his hind legs, "I've got it! Stuffy needs to get a job."

Then Tiny began to think again. "What kind of job? Teaching at a school? No, he couldn't teach, he's a bear. Unlike me, he's not so clever, but he could become a caretaker: that's a good idea, he definitely could protect the children and the school from bad people. But if he became grumpy, he probably would frighten the children. If he became hungry and there wasn't any food, he might become really grumpy and eat one of the children or maybe two of three, or worse still he might even eat a teacher. No I don't think Stuffy would be good at working at a school. I will have to think of something else when my tiny brain is rested."

After Tiny had a tiny brain rest he began to think again. "Perhaps I could find him a lady bear, then he would have a girl friend. And then later they could get married, then he wouldn't depend on me anymore. But he would have to take care of her and get food for her, unless she was a wild bear who was good at hunting. But I would prefer him to find a nice tame bear so he wouldn't go back to living in the wild. Oh! This is so complicated. There must be an answer I will have to keep thinking with my tiny brain until I find a solution."

By this time Stuffy had woken up from his nap and of course he was hungry.

"Let's go and find some honey or fishes," he growled.

"I guess that's a good idea," replied Tiny hoping they would find some food or he would have a brain wave before too long. So off they went not only to search for honey and fishes, but also to have another tiny adventure.

"I was thinking, that perhaps I could find you a

job," said Tiny as they were walking through the forest,

Stuffy looked at Tiny with a curious expression on his face "A job! What kind of Job?" ("I bet you have never seen a bear with a curious look on its face; I know I haven't, but it really was happening.")

"I'm not sure yet, but I'm thinking about it and I am open to suggestions," replied Tiny.

"I'm not sure if I want or need a job. After all, you are taking care of me by showing me how to live this tame life," growled Stuffy.

"But you'll have to branch out on your own sometime," replied Tiny. "I can't take care of you forever."

"So you want to get rid of me already?" growled back Stuffy who was now looking angry.

"No, that's not true, but you are big and strong enough to take care of yourself. I don't want to rush you, but I think that if you had a good and interesting job and then you could provide for yourself and then perhaps you will meet a nice lady bear who is looking for a handsome bear like you for a husband that will take care of her and one day you could become a proud father of some beautiful bear cubs."

"Do your really think that's possible that I could get a good job and find a beautiful bride?" asked Stuffy looking very interested and excited.

"I don't see why not, but let's find you a job first," replied Tiny.

So off they went continuing on their tiny adventure excited to see what was in store for them.

"Jobs for bears are rather limited. You can't work

in a store as a salesclerk. You can't be a politician. You could go to a zoo, but that's not really a proper job," explained Tiny as they continued their walk looking for food.

Suddenly they came across a beehive. "Great!! Honey comb for us. I'm sure after we have eaten I will be able to think more clearly," exclaimed Tiny.

I'm not sure about my thinking, but I do know my tummy will feel better after I have eaten," replied Stuffy with his usual growl.

It wasn't long before they found the honeycomb and began to enjoy their feast; even though the bees were not too happy and tried to sting them which didn't work because bears have thick fur coats which protects them from being stung, but it makes them hot in the summer.

"I feel stuffed and sleepy," growled Stuffy with a big yawn.

"So do I." said Tiny sleepily.

So as it was a warm day and their tummies were full of honey, they decided to take a nap under a shady tree before they continued their tiny adventure.

An hour or so later, Tiny woke up with an idea.

"Wake up! Wake up! Stuffy, you could get a job at a circus."

"A circus?" asked Stuffy with another big yawn.

"Yes a circus, but you will have to be trained to do tricks."

"What kind of tricks?"

"Jumping through hoops, standing on your head,

picking out numbers on cards, riding a tricycle," said Tiny excitedly.

"What's a tricycle?" asked Stuffy looking puzzled.

"It's a kid's bicycle. It has a big wheel in the front with pedals and two little wheels at the back." replied Tiny.

"But I'm not a kid or even a cub, I'm old and too big to ride a tricycle and probably too old to learn tricks," declared Stuffy.

"How old are you? asked Tiny.

"I don't know, but I must be very old, look how big I am!"

"Just because you're big doesn't mean you're really old, anyway they make special tricycles and bicycles for bears. And you could learn to balance and finally be able to ride a two wheeler. And they might have a lovely lady bear working at the circus who is lonely and you could meet her and perhaps she could be the one for you," replied Tiny excitedly.

"Hang on! You're going a bit too fast for me. I will have to think about it. Also I will need to find out how much this job pays."

"Well I don't think they will give you money, they will probably just give you food," explained Tiny.

"But they might have food I don't like. Would they have a cafeteria where I can line up with the other animals and choose my favorite foods?" ask Stuffy hopefully.

"I doubt it. Perhaps you're not cut out for the circus. I guess you like to be free and independent," said

Tiny thoughtfully.

"Well I don't mind trying the circus for a week or two and see if it will work out for me." replied Stuffy.

"I think it would take longer than a week or two to train you. It might take two or three years. Also you wouldn't be allowed to leave if you were not a happy because they would own you. If it didn't work out they would probably sell you to a zoo. Of course if you were really lucky they might donate you to an animal refuge center." explained Tiny as best he could.

"Well it doesn't sound too encouraging. What's an animal refuge center?" ask Stuffy.

It's like a retirement home for old people. They just sit around not doing much, and waiting to be fed," explained Tiny as best he could.

"Well I'm not that old. There is still plenty of life in me yet," growled Stuffy indignantly.

"Then we will have to think of something else. I'm sure we will come up with a solution sooner or later," declared Tiny hopefully.

So off they went in the afternoon sun, chatting away and think about all their possibilities.

Things went very well for the two bears for the next few days. They found plenty of honey and were able to fill up many jars. In fact, Tiny needed to go to see if he could find some more jars.

Just outside a village, Tiny discovered a little open air market and it wasn't long before he came across a stall where there were lots of empty jars for sale.

Tiny was very polite, "Excuse me, I'm a bear and

bears don't usually have or use money, but I'm interested in some of your jars."

The stall owner opened her mouth, closed it and opened it again staring at Tiny in amazement, "Did you speak or was that a ventriloquist?"

Tiny being very clever for a bear knew what a ventriloquist was, even though Stuffy didn't.

"No! that was me speaking," he said proudly.

"Oh My!" said the stall owner, where did you learn to talk?"

"I was always able to talk, I'm a very special bear from Lilliput. And I am able to trade some of our extra honey for some of your empty jars if you are willing?"

"Yes! Yes! Certainly." said the stall owner not wanting to make the bears angry and still excited about hearing Tiny talk.

So it was quite an event to see Tiny the talking bear at the market trading jars for honey. Even Stuffy said a few growley words much to the delight of the stall owner. She would have something to tell her friends about, if they believed her.

Well as you can imagine, Tiny and Stuffy caused quite a stir and many children came around and watched the two bears in delight. They had never seen such a thing, but they kept their distance, because they were not sure about Stuffy as he was so big and fierce looking. Of course Stuffy originally being a wild bear still looked wild sometimes and could be a little frightening. But he was learning to become more friendly like Tiny and was trying very hard to show it. Finally the two bears waved goodbye to the children, collected their jars and made their way back to their den.

When they arrived back they immediately started to fill up their extra jars with honey and store them away in a safe place. They certainly had plenty of honey now and it was quite possible that they would soon find another beehive and collect even more honey.

"If you want me to work I could open up a honey shop," suggested Stuffy excitedly.

Tiny looked at Stuffy with interest, "Where would you do that?"

"I'm not sure! I guess we could see if there are any shops for sale," growled Stuffy screwing up his face and thinking very hard.

"That might be expensive and we don't have any money to start us off. On the other hand, we could go back to the market and see if we can find a stall to put our honey on," explained Tiny, pleased with himself for thinking of such a good answer.

"Do you believe we will have enough honey to sell and do you think people will come just to buy honey?" asked Stuffy.

"Probably not! We will have to think of other things to sell. Also we will need to find out what we would call our stall, something like, 'Bears Honey Shop,' or 'Honey Pot' or 'Bears Antique Honey Pot Shop,' perhaps even 'Tiny's Treasures,'" suggested Tiny.

"Well, I would like my name put in there somewhere," growled Stuffy.

"I know, let's sit down, eat a jar of honey and

have another think. I'm sure we can come up with a good plan."

"I like good plans," growled Stuffy reaching for the honey jar and sitting down.

So they both sat down and ate their honey and thought hard.

After a while Stuffy had a brain wave. "We could also sell stuffed animals, preferably stuffed bears."

That's a great idea. "Stuffed Bears and Honey," said Tiny.

"How about Stuffy's stuffed Bears and Honey."

"I want my name in there as well and you can't have stuffed honey," replied Tiny.

"We could call it Stuffy's Bears & Tiny's Honey Stall, or perhaps shop rather than stall, it sound more fancy,'" explained Stuffy.

"You are learning fast to become civilized," said Tiny approvingly, "but I think I should be mentioned first; Tiny's Honey and Stuffy's stuffed Bears shop."

After a lot more thinking and plenty of discussion they finally agreed on a name, Tiny and Stuffy's Toy Bears and Honey Shop." Now they had another problem, whether to sell the honey and toy bears separately or together. "Buy a toy bear and get a free tiny jar of honey." or "Buy a tiny jar of honey and get a free toy bear." They finally decided to change it weekly and take turns. So off they went back to the market to see if they could rent or find a stall to start their business.

As they were walking back to the market they suddenly thought about where to get the toys bears from.

"We can make them! Bears making bears, who can do better than that?" exclaimed Stuffy.

"You're right! If bears can't make toy bears then they are not worth their weight in fur." exclaimed Tiny.

"If we can stuff our tummies with food then we can stuff toy bears with stuffing and sell them easily," growled Stuffy getting excited at the thought of it.

When they returned to the market they found the manager and sure enough he had a spare stall they could rent. He even let them rent it free for a month to see how they would do, even though he was somewhat puzzled having talking bears selling goods at his market. So now Tiny and Stuffy were on their way to becoming successful business bears or bear shopkeepers. I hope we find out if they become successful in the next chapter.

Chapter Four
Tiny and Stuffy Open Their Shop

Tiny and Stuffy were excited with their new stall. They were allowed to place it under a nice shady tree in a corner of the market. They weren't too close to the other stalls as some stall owners didn't like the smell of bears and others were a little frightened of being too near to Tiny and Stuffy. But after a while when people found out how friendly the bears were, they began to visit them to say "Hi." Some even began to buy their goods.

Before the two bears began to sell their stuffed or toy bears, they bought some materials and stuffing from some of the other stall holders. Fortunately they were able to sell enough jars of honey to pay for the material. One kind lady lent them a sewing machine to make the toy bears with. Imagine seeing bears using a sewing machine and making stuffed animals. They mostly made bears, but they also made a few smaller animals with some of the material that was left over. After the children became accustomed to seeing the "Bear and Honey Stall' they would pull their parents over to see the bears and some even wanted to pet Tiny as he was really small. Tiny wasn't too keen on being petted, but he put up with it, because it was good for business and he made sure that they at least bought one of his tiny jars of honey.

"It's fun and great having these people buy our goods, but I would like to have some bears come and buy honey and toy bears for their children," said Stuffy.

"But bears don't usually come and shop at markets. Also if they did where would they get the money from?" asked Tiny.

Stuffy look at Tiny and nodded his head, "Oh they have money. They find it when people go camping and lose it in the woods. I know some wild bears that have found gold coins. They like to keep them as they are so shiny, but I'm not sure what they do with the paper money that they find."

"My Oh My! I'm learning about wild bears as much as you are learning about tame bears. This is very interesting," replied Tiny squeezing a purse with his paw, "This is where I keep my money."

"Then we have to think of a way for them to know where to come. Perhaps we could make fliers and have them posted on some trees in the forest." suggested Stuffy.

"You mean printing fliers telling the bears where to come to buy toy bears and honey?"

"Absolutely, Tiny."

"But wild bears can't read, so it wouldn't work Stuffy," stated Tiny.

"Well, that's not altogether true."

"What do you mean Stuffy?" asked Tiny

"Some wild bears can read. Most of the common bears can't, but the royal wild bears and many of their relatives and friends read quite well."

"How did they learn to do that? I'm sure they did-n't attend public school."

"Oh No! Who ever heard of bears going to school! They have private tutors, replied Stuffy.

"Where did they find them?" asked Tiny, who was not only very clever for a bear, but was also very inquisitive. That's probably why he was so clever, be-cause he asked lots of questions and learned a lot. You should always ask lots of questions, then you could be-come very clever like Tiny, but if you don't you may grow up ignorant.

"Sometimes they advertise, but mostly they have connections with people who know that some bears can talk. And if they can talk, they can also be taught to read and write. Mind you, it's not so easy for bears to write because they have such big paws, which are great for catching fish, but not so great for holding a pen or pen-cil." explained Stuffy.

By this time, Tiny was wondering if Stuffy was cleverer than he was. He shook his head, "No, it can't be. He is a wild bear and I'm a tame bear. I guess he must be good and special for a wild bear. And come to think of it, I'm must be really clever for choosing him to be my friend," he thought.

"So do you want to have fliers printed?" asked Stuffy.

"I guess so, but we will have to find a printers that serve bears. Also as a safety measure, we need to invite the bears to come to our stall when the market is closed to the people, which is on a Monday," replied Tiny.

Stuffy wrinkled up his nose, "Ok, we will do that. Now going to the printers could be a problem because we could frighten them. If we find one, perhaps they might mistake us for people dressed up in bear skins for a party or a carnival."

"That's a thought, but it makes me shudder thinking about people dressed up in bear skins, it might be one of your ancestors." said Tiny.

"Why not one of your ancestors?' asked Stuffy.

"Because we all came from Lilliput and they would be too small for people to dress up in; unless they were little children. On the other hand, I think the bear skins that people dress up in aren't real, they are just made like stuffed bears," replied Tiny.

"Well, that's a relief. Although I heard a rumor that some nasty people have real bear skins for rugs on their floor," said Stuffy.

"If that's true, that's disgusting," cried Tiny. "Well, let's go and find a printers and tell them we are dressed up for a carnival."

So off Tiny and Stuffy went to find a printers to print their fliers. As they rumbled along towards their destination they were fortunate to find a printers just on the edge of town. They were glad about this, because bears don't usually walk around in a town. People might become alarmed and call the police, or the animal control, or a circus, or the zoo. They obviously didn't want to get arrested, or shot, or captured.

They did give the people who worked at the printers a bit of a shock, but when they said they were dressed up for a carnival and wanted the fliers printed to sell honey and teddy bears, the people believed them. They were told to return in a couple of hours and they would print two hundred fliers for them.

"This seems to be working quite well. And we have enough money to pay for the fliers," said Tiny happily, checking his purse around his neck.

"Yes, then we will need a hammer and some nails to post them up on the trees in the forest, said Stuffy.

Tiny looked around and to his surprise there was a hardware store just two doors down from the printers.

"Well, what do you know? Things are really going well for us today."

I hope the people in the hardware store will also think we are people dressed in bear suits," said Stuffy keeping his claws crossed for luck.

"I think they will; we will soon found out," said Tiny as they pushed open the door to the store.

"Help! Help! A bear and her cub has just come through the door," cried a shop assistant with a terrified look on her face and she ducked under the counter.

"No! No! We are just dressed up for a carnival," said Tiny.

"Yes! Yes! We are pretending. We are dressed like bears," growled Stuffy.

The shop assistant peeped out from behind the counter where she had been hiding, "Well, you certainly could have fooled me. You look so real. You had me worried for a moment. How can I help you?"

"We need a hammer and some nails," said Tiny.

"Yes please! We need to put some fliers up, growled Stuffy.

34

"Right away!" said the shop assistant, handing the two bears a hammer and a box of nails.

As the bears walked out of the store with their hammer and nails, the shop assistant began to tell the others in the store how real the bears seemed. "They even smelt like bears, but they must have been people, after all everyone knows that bears don't go shopping and they certainly can't talk."

It didn't take very long for Tiny and Stuffy to go through the woods nailing up fliers on some of the big trees.

"There! That should do it," cried Stuffy in his growley voice, nailing the last flier to a very large tree.

"So all we need to do now is to wait for all the customers to come," said Tiny with a pleased look upon his face, "I do hope I have enough honey to sell."

"I'm glad you thought of inviting the bears to come on Tuesday when the market is not officially open. Come to think of it, do we have a spare flier to look at to make sure it was accurate?" asked Stuffy as they made their way back to their den.

"No, but I remember what I told you to write on the flier, as I have a great memory for a bear."

"Bears! Everywhere! Come to Tiny and Stuffy's shop at the open air market just on the edge of town and see all the jars of honey we have for sale and the special stuffed toy bears and animals for your cubs to play with. Open for business on Monday 8.00 am—4.00 pm if you can tell the time. For those who can't, check where the sun is or come after your breakfast. We don't take credit cards only money, or we might trade something."

"I thought you said it was Tuesday," growled Stuffy looking alarmed.

"No! I told you Monday was the day when the market was closed," replied Tiny.

With that both bears rushed back to the woods to take the fliers down, but it was too late; most of them had been taken back to the bear's dens.

"I shouldn't have trusted a wild bear to do the complicated part," thought Tiny. He didn't want to say it out loud as he might make Stuffy really angry and when Stuffy gets angry he gets scary.

"I know! We can put up a notice at the entrance warning the customers that bears will be coming to our stand," said Stuffy.

"But wouldn't that keep most of the people away and the shop owners would be very angry with us for losing their business?" replied Tiny, "I have an idea. I will go, talk to the manager, for I think we can work out a solution."

The manager was quite concerned about all the bears coming to the open market at first, but Tiny made an excellent suggestion.

"I think, Mr. Manager that we could make a special entrance for the bears to get to our stall so they won't pass by all the other stalls and scare the customers and the stall venders. We can put up a notice and make a special path for the bears going to our stall without them entering through the main entrance."

"But bears can't read and they may go through the wrong entrance," replied the manager.

"Some bears can read" growled Stuffy.

"And we can put a poster up of a bear so they will know where to go," added Tiny.

"Well, I guess it's worth a try, but mind you, if they don't stay on the right path and scare all the people I will have to call the sheriff."

So it was agreed by all that they would try out that plan and hope and pray that it would work. Now it was up to Tiny and Stuffy to find a poster of a bear and put some writing on it. So it was back to the printers again.

"What will the printer people think this time when we tell them what we want on the poster?" said Stuffy looking concerned.

"We will have to tell them that it's all part of the carnival. They will think it will be like a fancy dress party and those that dress up like bears have to stay together; I hope," declared Tiny.

When Tiny and Stuffy arrived back at the printers they were able to find them a nice large poster of a bear. They didn't want to tell the printers that they made a mistake with the fliers as they were embarrassed. It's one thing for people to make a silly mistake and feel embarrassed, but for bears it's much worse. Don't ask me why? Because I don't know, but I've been told on good authority, that bears hate being embarrassed. The printer had no problem with sticking large letters on the poster which said, "Bears Only! This Way Please!" They also made a few more smaller bears signs for them so that the bears wouldn't get lost and they would be able to find their way to Tiny's and Stuffy's stall.

Tiny and Stuffy quickly returned to the open air market and found posts and trees to nail their signs onto.

Three days later, which was a Tuesday they waited patiently for the bears to come and buy their honey and stuffed animals.

Chapter Five
Market Day for the Bears

"Do you know what we should have done," said Tiny thoughtfully as they waited for the bears to come and shop.

"No! What?" replied Stuffy.

"We should have bought a CD player and a CD of the song, *'The Teddy Bear's Picnic.'*"

"Do they know that song?" asked Stuffy.

"I'm sure some of them do, it's very old. Let me see, how do the words go? I think I remember some."

"If you go down to the woods today, you'd better go in disguise.

If you go down to the woods today, you're in for a big surprise.

For every bear that ever there was, is there today for certain because, today's the day the teddy bears have their picnic." "And there's a lot more words to that song," said Tiny getting excited.

"I wonder if the kids who read or hear about our adventures know that song?" asked Stuffy.

"Well, if they don't, they should certainly get to know it. Let's hope their parents will find the words and music on the internet or somewhere and get it for them. My parents used to sing it to me when I was little," said Tiny.

"When you were little? That's a joke, you still are," guffawed Stuffy with his growley voice.

"I bet you don't know what the internet is and what CD's are, Even though I'm littler than you, I am cleverer than you. I'm the brains and you're the brawn," said Tiny.

"Well we make a good team then. And you will never get bigger, but I will become cleverer, since I'm learning to become a tame bear," declared Stuffy."

So we never found out in this chapter if Stuffy really knew what a CD player was and what CD's were. But rest assured, I'm sure he eventually found out because he was so anxious to learn. So remember learning is good for you, even though sometimes it's hard and can be a pain in the b—tt to a lot of children.

"If I had thought of a CD player the bears would have been able to follow the music as well as the signs. Maybe next time we have a sale for the bears we can do that," sighed Tiny.

Suddenly Tiny and Stuffy saw a company of bears coming down the path to their stall.

"Quick Stuffy! Get ready! We have customers," cried Tiny excitedly.

"I'm ready!" growled Stuffy, getting all his stuffed animals out on view.

As the bears came by the stall they ogled at the honey and the bear cubs ogled at the toys and the honey.

It wasn't long before the bears were buying the stuffed animals and the honey. It was a strange sight to see these bears; quite a number had silver coins in the paws, and a few with gold coins. Also there were a lot that had paper money. I would have thought that bears wouldn't even know what paper money was, but you'd be surprised, a lot of them knew. Tiny was changing ten silver coins to one gold coin. They ended up at the end of the day with six gold coins, twenty seven silver coins, a big wad of dollar bills and quite a number of quarters, nickels and dimes. It was amazing to think how those bears had all that money which goes to show how many people are careless with their belongings when the go camping in the woods.

Some of the bears had some fish that they wanted to trade, but they were a bit too smelly for Tiny, although Stuffy originally being a wild bear wouldn't have minded trading. In the end he decided not to do it, as they would be really smelly by the end of the day. He could had eaten the fish raw like most wild bears do, but he had gotten to like it cooked, which Tiny always did when they had fish for supper.

There were some squabbles amongst some of the bear cubs. The girl cubs wanted cuddly stuffed animals and the boy cubs wanted action stuffed animals which is a bit hard to find. Stuffy almost rushed down to a *Wal-Mart* to buy some action figures for the boy cubs, but Tiny talked him out of it and told he to try *Toys R US* instead. No! That's not true, I'm just teasing the boys and girls reading this story. But listen! Everything else is true; if you can use your imagination.

Even a few brave people came over and bought

some honey while the bears were there. I think they were curious to see bears go shopping as they were using their cell phone cameras to take pictures. Some of the little cubs stood on their hind legs and growled at them pretending they were dangerous. The mother bears seemed to be amused at seeing their cubs showing off to the people. Most of the father bears weren't there. Just like people, lady bears seem to enjoy shopping more than the men bears.

Little Children Bears With Their Toys

As it was getting near closing and most of the bears had left or were leaving, Tiny said, "Well Stuffy, we had a really good day today, didn't we?"

"Yes we did! I can't wait till next Tuesday for them to come back again. Oh dear! We didn't say this would be every Tuesday on the fliers."

"You are right. We will have to have some more fliers printed if we want them to come back again and maybe we should change it to Monday. Perhaps we should check with the market manager and see what he thinks? Well, we learn by our mistakes. It's still been a good day and we made a lot of sales," said Tiny.

"You are going to have to find some more honey and I'm going to have to buy some more material and make some more animals and bears." said Stuffy.

Tiny looked at Stuffy and gave him a bear smile, "First of all, after closing our stall, I'm going to go back to our den and see how many jars of honey we have left to eat and how many to sell. Then we will eat and then we can have a little rest and tomorrow I will go and see if I can find a bee hive and you can go to the lake and see if you can catch any nice fresh fish for our supper."

So it was agreed and that's exactly what they did. So let's all hope and trust that our two bears will continue to be successful in their honey and stuffed bear business for a long time to come. And you know what? I believe we will find them very successful as more stories of their adventures are written.

Chapter Six
Tiny The Bear Gives Some Wise Advice

Tiny had been dreaming about their business and how to make it even more successful. He had some new ideas about using a CD player. When he got up from his nap he decided to take a tiny stroll. Bears don't usually take strolls, but Tiny is not a "usual bear" he is an "unusual bear" as we all well know. Stuffy had gone fishing, so Tiny was all by himself. He was thinking about how good their shop was doing with the stuffed bears and tiny jars of honey when he almost bumped into a little girl. "Excuse me!" said Tiny.

"That's alright, I was hoping to bump into you. Well not literally bump into you, but to find you and talk to you," she replied.

"A lot of children want to meet me and talk to me. I think they are excited about meeting a talking bear from Lilliput."

"I don't just want to talk to you, but I want you to eat me," she replied.

"Oh no! This has happened before. You are too big for me to eat and I do prefer honey and fish. Remember I only have a tiny tummy."

"What about your friend Stuffy? I'm told he is a big bear and he can be quite fierce. I bet he could eat me. He could probably eat me up fast; in a few minutes." said the little girl, beginning to cry.

"You don't have a funny name, do you?" asked Tiny.

"I can't remember my name, that's why I am so unhappy; perhaps I don't even exist," she cried.

"How come you can't remember your name?"

"Because I'm called by so many names by different people, that I can't remember what my real name is anymore or even if I ever had one."

"What kind of names do they call you?" asked Tiny.

"Almost every name you can think of."

"Such as?" persisted Tiny with his questions.

"Ugly, stupid, idiot, smelly. stinky, horrible, dumb, useless, nasty, rat-face, bug-eyed, spotty-face, and lots more," she said tearfully.

"Oh Dear!" said Tiny looking alarmed, "what does your mother call you?"

"I'm trying to remember, I know it's not nice," she said wrinkling up her brow trying to think.

"Oh please try to think hard, it might help," said Tiny.

With that she screwed her little face up with thinking so hard. After a few minutes she said, "Well I know it wasn't any of the others I just mentioned." Then she began to count on her fingers all the names she had been called. Then she sat down took her shoes and socks off and began to count on all her toes as well. "She didn't call me any of them," she said shaking her head, "But I know she called my something nasty. She suddenly jumped up, "I remember she called me loser."

"Loser! Why did she call you loser?" asked Tiny.

"Because that's my name," she said in a way that seemed to obvious to her.

"Is that your first name?" asked Tiny.

"Of course not, that's my last name," she replied.

Just then Stuffy rumbled in with a paw full of fresh fish. "Look what I got!" he said in his growley voice.

The little girl jumped up and ran over to Stuffy and fell at his feet. "Please! Please! Mr. Bear, will you eat me?"

Stuffy looked very surprised, "Why does she want me to eat her?" he asked, looking at Tiny.

Tiny explained the situation to Stuffy and it didn't take long for Stuffy to understand as he was fast becoming a tame bear.

"Little girl, I don't think it would be a good idea for me to eat you and I think Tiny can help your problem in a much better way than being eaten," he said politely with his gruff voice. Stuffy was so quickly becoming more tame that even his voice was changing from growley to gruffy.

"I think I can help you little girl, because I was able to help a little boy a long time ago that wanted me to eat him, because he didn't like his name." said Tiny.

"Well, I certainly hope so. I guess being eaten is not such a good idea," she replied.

"Tiny went over to the little girl and looked right into her face. "So tell me, can you remember your first name?"

"I think I can remember if I try," she screwed up her face again, then wrinkled her brow and thought very hard. "It's Lily, no it's Lulu, no it's Lucy. Yes, 'Lucy Loser' that's my name. I also remember my mother had to call me by my last name, because my second grade teacher never calls her students by their first name, only their last name. This was the rules so when I went into her class, she made my mom introduced me as 'Loser' and everyone laughed and started calling me a loser. Then it went from bad to worse as the kids began to add all those other nasty names to call me," she then burst into tears.

"But you don't have to be a loser Lucy, just because that's your last name. You can become a winner," declared Tiny with Stuffy nodding his big head in agreement.

"You really think so?" asked Lucy.

"Absolutely, but first I need to ask you some more questions," said Tiny.

"What kind of questions?" asked Lucy.

"Why do your wear that funny old hat on your head which covers most of your face and no one can see your hair?

"So people won't notice me."

"Why don't you want people to notice you Lucy?" asked Stuffy.

"If they don't notice me then perhaps they won't be mean and call me bad names," she replied.

"I don't think that's the answer to your problem. I think you should wash your face, brush your hair

("and teeth,") cried out Stuffy.
and make yourself look pretty and change your clothes
and you must get rid of that hat, said Tiny.

"Well I guess I could give it a try," said Lucy re-
moving her funny hat and there was the cutest face you
ever did see and beautiful curly locks came tumbling
down from under her hat

"Wow! You look like Goldilocks," cried Tiny.

"And we are the two bears. Sorry we have one
missing, I'm still waiting to find a wife," said Stuffy.

"I didn't know you knew about Goldilocks and the
three bears?" said Tiny.

"Well, I found your book and began to read it,"
replied Stuffy.

"So you can read now, that's great," cried Tiny.

"Well, the book has lots of pictures in it, so I kind
of guessed most of the story with reading some of the
little words and looking at the pictures. But I'm really trying, because I want to be able to read really well, especially for a bear." replied Stuffy proudly.

"That's great! I wish all the children today would
read a lot more and stop watching so many movies and
playing with video games," stated Tiny, who as you
know is very wise for a bear.

"Now this is what we want you to do Lucy. Go
home and clean yourself up, take a shower or bath, put
on a pretty outfit and comeback and see us. We are going to take you to see your second grade teacher,' said
Tiny.

"Yes! We need to speak to her," added Stuffy,
"Oh and don't forget to brush your teeth."

Tiny The Bear Gives Some Wise Advice

Lucy Loser

"Oh My! This will be interesting," shouted Lucy as she run off to do what our two bears told her.

A couple of hours later Lucy returned. Oh my! Did she look different.

"Wow!" said the bears together, "You look so pretty."

"And you're smiling," added Tiny.

Lucy now looked very cute and cool looking.

Lucy Loser

"Remember, just because your last name is *Loser* doesn't make you one," explained Tiny.

"Are we going to see the teacher?" asked Stuffy.

"Yes! But we must find out whether she's at the school, or at her home." replied Tiny.

"My teacher is probably still at the school, because she works on the children's homework for the next day and she looks after a few children that stay late until their parents get off from work and come to collect them," explained Lucy.

"Good! Then let's go and catch her before she leaves," said Tiny.

So off they went to the school, with an excited Lucy leading the way. What a strange sight to see a little girl walking along followed by two bears busy chatting to her.

They finally arrived at the almost deserted school. They followed Lucy inside and went straight to her classroom. Lucy asked them to wait outside until she spoke to Miss Manners her schoolteacher. She wanted to explain about bringing some visitors.

Lucy knocked on the door of the classroom,

"Come in" a voice said. Miss Manners stared at Lucy. "Oh it's you Loser. I didn't recognized you at first you look so different. A lot better I think," she said, as she peered through her spectacles, "Why are you here after hours?"

"I have two friends that need to talk to you, Miss Manners," Lucy said.

"They are not children are they? I have to put up with the little brats all day and don't want you bringing in your little friends to see me."

No, they aren't children, although one of them is little," replied Lucy.

"Very well, show them in."

Lucy went to the door and opened it.

Tiny The Bear Gives Some Wise Advice

Miss Manners

"You can come in now," she called.

The next thing that happened was quite funny to see. Miss Manners suddenly gave one leap and she was on top of a desk, then she gave another leap and landed on top of a book cupboard. She crouched on the top of it trembling. How she did that with two leaps we will never know, but she did it. For the first time in her life, (apart from when she was a baby) she couldn't speak. Her mouth was opening and shutting, but no words would come out and her eyes were wide with horror.

Finally she managed to stutter out some words, "B,B,B.Bears!" she screamed, "C,C,C,C, Call someone!"

"It's alright, Miss Manners. They are my friends, they won't hurt you; they just want to talk to you," said Lucy trying not to giggle too much.

Tiny looked up at Miss Manners, "She's right we won't hurt you we just want to talk to you."
Miss Manners shook her head from side to side, stuck her fingers in her ears and massaged them, rubbed her eyes, and pinched herself,

"I must be dreaming! No! I'm having a nightmare! No! I'm going mad, I've been working too hard."

"You are not dreaming, having a nightmare or going mad. We are real and we can talk," said Stuffy in is gruff voice.

"Oh No! Now they are both talking. I need to see the doctor." cried Miss Manners.

During this time Lucy was trying to stop giggling at the strange sight of Miss Manners crouching on top of the cupboard.

"What is you first name?" asked Tiny.

"M'M'M' Molly," stammered Miss Manners.

"Molly Manners, that's not a bad name," said Stuffy.

"So why do you just use your last name and call everyone else by their last names?" asked Tiny.

"B'B'B' Because I like good manners, and I don't want to get too close to the children by calling them by their first names. They just need to learn good manners," she replied beginning to get her composure back.

"Well we are going to call you Molly, if that's alright?" said Stuffy.

"C' Certainly! Certainly!" said Miss Manners who was still shaking a little.

"And you also need to call Miss Loser by her first name, which is Lucy. In fact, you should be friendly with the children and learn to call them all by their first names and not just their last names."

"Yes! Yes!" I will! I will! replied Miss Manners willing to do everything the bears suggested.

"Did you know that when you introduced Lucy to her class as 'Loser' everyone laughed and made fun of her? said Tiny very sternly.

"And all the children began to make up all kinds of bad names to call her which made her so depressed that she wanted me to eat her," explained Stuffy.

"Oh dear! I didn't realize that had happened. I will make sure that the children in her class will treat *Loser,* sorry Lucy, with great respect, as we all should," promised Miss Molly, which we will now call her.

"Good! So if Lucy has to come back and ask me to eat her, I will come and eat you instead," said Stuffy with a good loud growl.

And with that, they left the school and Miss Manners, sorry Molly, while Lucy was still giggling.

"I'm not sure Stuffy if you should have said you would come and eat her," said Tiny.

"I know, it just came out. I guess I got carried away, I've still got some of the wild bear left in me," growled Stuffy with a smile.

"Well I think you both did great and I know now that I can be a winner. And it helps a lot when you have two great bears as your friends," and with that, Lucy gave them both such a big hug that they were almost bear hugs and she went off happily skipping down the road.

Molly Manners climbed down from the high book cupboard onto the chair and back onto the floor. She sat down on the floor and said, "Oh! I have just had an Epiphany. God sent two angels dressed up as bears to teach me a lesson. I will never be the same again."

And she never was!

So Tiny the wise bear, was also able to help a little girl as he was able to help a little boy in the first story. And because he is such a nice, wise and kind bear who rescued Stuffy from being too wild and made him his best friend, Stuffy also became a great help to the little girl Molly, as Tiny was to Flippin.

Chapter Seven
Tiny and Stuffy Have a Special Party

Tiny felt it was time to see how Flippin Aweful and Lucy Loser were doing so he invited them over for a little party.

"I want to see how you are doing and bring any of your friends," he said on his new cell phone. " I don't know how he knew their phone numbers, but he probably looked them up in the telephone directory. Remember, Tiny is very clever for a bear.

He and Stuffy decorated their den really nicely and they put out lots of honey with nice fresh bread to eat for their guests. Eventually Flippin showed up with two friends and Lucy also brought three friends. One of their friends also brought a friend as well. Their friends were curious to see talking bears, even though they were a little scared.

"Welcome! Welcome! Please come in," said Stuffy in his gruff voice.

"Thank You," chorused the visitors in a polite manner, cautiously looking around to find a safe place to sit.

"Please sit here next to me," said Tiny looking at two of the visitors.

"You others can sit near me," growled Stuffy much to their consternation. Soon everyone was settled

Rachael Ragamuffin

Lucy Loser with Penny Pincher, Theresa Teaser & Sarah Silly.

and Tiny began to talk. "Lucy, please introduce your friends."

"This is Rachael Ragamuffin," said Lucy pointing to a very scruffy looking girl.

"This is Sarah Silly," said Lucy again, pointing to a little girl that kept giggling all the time. "And this is Penny Pincher," pointing to a little girl who was clutching very tightly to her purse.

"Hmm! Very interesting names," stated Tiny looking as though he was getting ready to ask plenty of questions.

"Now Flippin, please introduce us to your friends."

"This is William Winn, but everyone calls him Willie."

"Interesting! Willie Winn or Willie Wont?"

The little boy jumped up, That's my problem everybody thinks I should win, but most of the time I don't! I just keep losing. I can't live up to my name." Then he burst into tears sobbing with his mouth wide open still full of the bread and honey that he had been eating.

"Calm down! I thought this was supposed to be a party; seems more like a 'pity party' to me," growled Stuffy.

"Yes we can't help you and fix your Boo Boo's if you don't stop sobbing," added Tiny.

And this is my friend, "Theresa Teaser" and she has real problems. She won't stop teasing and everyone is tired of her. She really lives up to her name," said Rachael Ragamuffin.

"Oh Dear! We have a lot of problem children at

Tiny and Stuffy have a special party

Flippin Aweful with Willie Winn and Donald Duck

our party!" exclaimed Tiny.

"Is there anymore kids with problems?" asked Stuffy with his usual growl.

"Just one more," answered Flippin. "This boy here has a funny name. His last name is Duck and his parents named him Donald."

"Donald Duck! Are you kidding me?" asked Tiny.

"Perhaps we'd better just eat all your friends and get it over with" suggested Stuffy, "although that's a lot of kids to eat, even for a big bear like me."

"No, we can't do that! We will have to help them all. So line up and then I will have you come into my office one by one." explained Tiny.

"I didn't know bears had offices." said Rachael, who was first in line.

"I didn't know bears counseled people," giggled Sarah, who was next in line.

"I hope it doesn't' cost anything," mumbled Penny, standing behind Sarah and still clutching her purse.

"I think maybe perhaps they can help me," said Donald waiting behind Penny.

"Quack! Quack!" teased Theresa, laughing at Donald and trying to tickle him.

"I know that I won't be helped, I'm already last in line. If I lived up to my name I would have been first in line," sobbed Willie, his mouth now half filled with the remains of the bread and honey.

"Tiny! I think you will need my help. We have a lot of work to do and we need a lot of wisdom. Perhaps we should see if we can get a wise Owl to help us," growled Stuffy, as he entered into their little office in their den.

As Rachael Ragamuffin was the first in line she entered the bears office. "This is going to be an easy one," said Tiny.

"Good! The easier the better," said Stuffy who wanted to get this whole thing over as quickly as possible so he could go the bed early.

"Why do you look like a ragamuffin? Are you so poor that you can't buy soap to wash with and nice clothes to wear?" asked Tiny.

"Just because your last name is Ragamuffin doesn't mean you have to look and behave like one," growled Stuffy.

Rachael's face went red, "I really don't know. I guess all my friends expect me to look like my name, so I'm trying to please them."

"Well you need to stop trying to be a people pleaser; ignore them and be your own person. I want to show you two pictures I took with my camera phone of Lucy Loser. I call them my before and after pictures," replied Tiny. With that he brought out his phone and showed Rachael.

"Oh My! What a difference! Do you think I could look like the second picture?" cried Rachael.

"Absolutely!" growled Stuffy.

"I didn't know bears had cell phones," whispered Penny Pincher.

"Especially with cameras; these bears are real neat," giggled Sarah Silly.

"Lucy! It would be good for you to help and encourage Rachael, as she is your friend." advised Tiny.

"I certainly will. I will treat her like a best friend," said Lucy.

"Oh thank you! Thank you. As soon as I have some money I will buy a nice outfit" said Rachael, beaming from ear to ear.

"Sarah, would you mind if I had Penny Pincher come before you?" asked Tiny.

Sarah giggled nervously, "I guess."

"I have a reason" said Tiny, "Penny Pincher come forward."

Penny came into the office still clutching her purse.

"Why are you holding your purse so tightly?" asked Tiny.

"I must take good care of my money, because I'm very poor," she replied.

Just at that moment she tripped over a chair and dropped her purse onto the floor. It burst open and instead of just a few cents or dollars, it was packed with money which spilt all over the floor. Believe me! Most of them were $100.00 bills, which was very unusual, especially for a little girl.

"Oh! You certainly live up to your name," growled Stuffy looking at Penny who was on the floor grabbing her money and stuffing it back into her purse and trying to hide it, so no one would know how rich she really was.

"I would like you to do me a tiny favor. It will help you to be a better person." said Tiny.

"What is this tiny favor that will make me a better person?" asked Penny, frantically stuffing her money back into her purse.

"You need to either give Rachael $300.00 or take her to a store and buy her a nice outfit."

"Oh Dear! Oh Dear! I don't know if I can afford to do that," replied Penny looking very agitated.

"But you must do something; if you don't want to be eaten," growled Stuffy.

"Alright! I will take Rachael to a store. There is a nice *'Thrift'* store near where I live and they have lots of used clothes. That's where I'll take her and I will pay for her outfit," Penny nervously replied.

Tiny got up and put his face close to Penny's. "Forget the *'Thrift'* store, you must take her to a nice store so she can have the best outfit that will make her look pretty and smart."

Penny screwed up her face, winced, and bit her lip, "Ok! Ok! I will do it. Even though I've never done anything like this before, I guess there is a first time for everything."

"And make sure it's not the last time you do anything like this, if you don't want to be eaten," growled Stuffy.

"You can't keep threatening the kids like that!" said Tiny.

"Well remember, I'm still a bit of a wild bear and anyway that's what I call 'tough love' and it does work," replied Stuffy.

"Penny! You mustn't live in fear that you don't

have enough. If you become generous it will come back to you. What you sow, you will reap," advised Tiny.

"Wow! He has a lot of wisdom for a bear, cried Willie. "Perhaps he will be able to help me even though I'm last in line. I hope he doesn't run out of wisdom before he gets to me."

"I will do as you say! I'm feeling better already," replied Penny.

"Well, lets hope you will still feel better when you pay for Rachael's outfit." growled Stuffy.

"So who's next?" asked Tiny.

"Me! Me! Me!" replied Sarah giggling.

"So why do you do what you do?" asked Stuffy.

"Because I do! Its fun," giggled Sarah.

"Do you know what serious is?" asked Tiny.

"No! and I don't want to!" giggled Sarah again.

"Why Not?" growled Stuffy.

"Because," giggled Sarah

"Because?" asked Tiny.

"Because! Because!" replied Sarah and went into fits of laughter.

"This is hopeless," growled Stuffy.

"Who is next?" asked Tiny

"I am! As soon as you're finished with goofy, giggly, gummy worm head," replied Theresa Teaser.

"I'm not a goofy gummy worm head. That's not nice to call me that," replied Sarah without giggling for the first time.

"Well if you act silly and stupid all the time people will get tired of you and call you nasty names," replied Tiny

"Well, she is nasty to everyone and she teases all the time. She even said to one boy, "Is that your real face or did your neck throw up?"

"So what did you do?" asked Tiny

"I just giggled and giggled, it was so funny." said Sarah.

"So you don't mind her teasing others as long as she doesn't tease you. And I thought you didn't care about anything or anyone,"

"Yes and you don't take anything seriously. Everything is just a laugh. All the time you just like to be silly," growled Stuffy.

"Well I guess I shouldn't, but that's my name and my friends expect me to be silly all the time."

"Is that right? Does everyone here like Sarah to be silly all the time?"

"No! We don't! It gets annoying; especially the continuous giggling," they all chorused together.

"Can I be silly sometimes?" asked Sarah looking hurt for the first time.

"I'm sure they won't mind sometimes. Just don't overdo it, just because your last name is Silly," said Tiny.

"That's fine! All of us like to be silly occasionally, after all we're kids," said Lucy smiling.

"And the same goes for you Theresa. Stop teasing everyone all the time and don't be mean," growled Stuffy.

"Yes! Especially if you don't want to be eaten. Oops! I shouldn't have said that, I'm not a wild bear," said Tiny.

"So we have two more to go!" growled Stuffy.

"Donald Duck! " cried Theresa, "I nearly said, 'Quack! Quack!' but I've changed, so I'm not saying it."

"Too late! You already said it," quacked Donald. Sorry! I'm writing the story and I'm being mean, I meant 'said' Donald.

"I wasn't trying to be a tease, I made a mistake. I will never say 'Quack' again in your presence. Oops! I said it again, said Theresa getting really frustrated. "Its very hard to break a bad habit, but I will keep on trying."

"So what shall we do with you Donald?" asked Tiny.

"Just stop people quacking at me for a start," replied Donald.

"Well, I have an idea! Go by the name Don and it won't sound so bad. Don Duck can swim like a duck,' said Stuffy.

" In fact I can. I can swim better than anyone and faster," said Don.

"Well, then take it as a complement. No one can swim as well as Don Duck. He is awesome. How about that for starters?" said Tiny.

"Yes! I will give it a try," said Donald smiling

"One more to go," growled Stuffy

"That's me! Last as usual," cried Willie.

"Don't be upset sometimes the best things are kept for last," Tiny replied in an encouraging way.

Flippin suddenly spoke up, "Yes! There is a story in the Bible about a wedding feast where the best wine was kept for last."

"I remember learning that at Sunday school

where Jesus turned the water into wine and it was the best wine." said Sarah.

"So what's that to do with me? I'm not wine!" said Willie.

"Well, your last name is Winn and that is pretty close to Wine, there is only one letter difference." explained Tiny.

"See yourself as 'Willie Wine' not 'Willie Whiner' You had become a Willie Whiner, because you couldn't be a Willie Winner." No more whining, just remember the last wine is best," advised Stuffy.

"I think I've got it." said Willie looking cheerful for the first time."

So after some more fun and some more bread and honey all the children went home changed for the better. Perhaps you have been changed for the better after reading these stories. Who would have thought that bears could be so wise and clever.

Perhaps we will hear more about the adventures of Tiny and Stuffy again one day.

The End.

Or is it?

Epilogue

By My Grandson Zion

After the party, Tiny and Stuffy went for a walk.

"I wish I could have some honey." growled Stuffy.

"Let's see if we can find some." said Tiny.

So for the next 30 minutes, Tiny and Stuffy went looking for some honey. Finally, Tiny said, "let's drop by my cousin's Sally's house."

"I hope she has some honey, but doesn't she live in a den?" growled Stuffy.

"Oh no, she is really civilized, she lives in a nice tiny house like the three bears' cottage," replied Tiny.

"Perhaps we could have a nice cottage built when we make enough money at our shop," said Stuffy excitedly.

'Yes! Perhaps!" replied Tiny as they rumbled along together. So, because of their hunger, Tiny and Stuffy walked all the way to Sally's tiny house, because they couldn't catch a bus being bears, which meant it was a long way for a tiny bear to walk. When they arrived, Tiny knocked on the door and Sally opened it. Stuffy and Sally's eyes met and it was love at first sight."

But that's another story.

Sally's House

Sally & Stuffy

Other Books By Pop Pop

David Walters known by his grandchildren as Pop Pop has written fifteen books.

Kids in Combat
Equipping the Younger Saints
Children Aflame
Worship fur Dummies
Radical Living
Anointing and You

(Six Illustrated Children's Bible Workbooks)
* Being a Christian *
* Fact or Fantasy *
* Armor of God *
* Fruit of the Spirit *
* Children's Prayer Manual *
* Gifts of the Spirit *

The Book of Funtastic Adventures
The 2nd Book of Funtastic Adventures

For more information on David Walters' books, DVD's & CD's please visit
goodnews.netministries.org
davidwaltersministry.com
funtasypublications.com
or write to
Good News Ministries
220 Sleepy Creek Rd. Macon, Georgia. 31210 USA
Phone: 478-757-8071 800-300-0136

Wee Willie Wannabe

This is the story of Wee Willie Wannabe. He was born in Australia and lived in the town of Walla Walla. Willie was still small and young, that's why he was known as Wee Willie. One day, Wee Willie Wannabe went for a walk and came across a Wallaby, which I'm sure you adults and most of you children know is a small Kangaroo. The Wallaby stared at Willie and Willie stared back at the Wallaby. Then a strange thing happened, the Wallaby spoke.

"Hi Mate. Who and what are you?"
Willie was taken back and very surprised as you don't often hear Wallabies talk. "Ur! I'm Wee Willie Wannabe and I'm a boy," he said.

"I can see that you're a boy, but what are you?" replied the Wallaby.

"I don't understand," said Willie Wannabe.

"Well, you said you are a Wannabe so what do you want to be?"

"That's my name," said Willie.

"Listen I'm a Wallaby, so I know who I am, but you are a Wannabe, so you don't know who you are or what you are yet. If you wannabe something, you must know what it is you wannabe! Get it!" said the Wallaby.

"I think so," said Wee Willie Wannabe.

"If you want to be something then you have to know what you are to begin with; then you can aim and what you wannabe. So what are you now?" asked the Wallaby.

"I'm a kid," said Willie.

"Well that's a start, so what do you want to be?"

"I want to be good at school," said Willie.

"Good at what?" asked the Wallaby.

"Math" replied Willie.

"What else?" asked the Wallaby. "Sports!" said Willie. "What kind of sports?" asked the Wallaby.

"Jumping," replied Willie.

"I can help you. I'll teach you,"

"Teach me math?" asked Willie.

"No! Who ever heard of a Wallaby teaching math? I can teach you to jump like a Wallaby or maybe a Kangaroo," explained the Wallaby.

"You would really do that for me?" asked Willie.

"Sure!" replied the Wallaby.

"When?" asked Willie"

"Right now and for the next ten weeks," said the Wallaby.

So for the next ten weeks Willie Wannabe learned how to jump like a Wallaby. Although he didn't quite jump as good as a kangaroo, he still became the best jumper in his school; not only in his school, but in the whole town and for miles around. Even the fully grown men couldn't jump as high and as far as Willie, so little Willie Wannabe became famous as Willie Wallaby the great jumper. So don't let your name, a couple of letters, or what other people say about you, hinder your chances of achieving your destiny. It only took three letters and determination to change Willie Wannabe into Willy Wallaby. And do you know he even improved at math. The same could happen to you!

Pop Pop.